EMERGENCY SERVICE VOLUNTEERS:
HOW TO GET THEM
and KEEP THEM!

SALLY STEWARD

Published 2014

Publisher: Sally Steward

Graphic Design & Layout: Melissa Caron - Go-Enki.com

Editing: Richard Burian - Go-Enki.com

Leadership, Emergency Services

Sally's passion and enthusiasm for volunteering in emergency services is contagious. Not only is she an experienced Firefighter and Community Educator, she also takes the time to mentor and train those around her. Sally has an adept understanding of leadership and the challenges of those in emergency services. Having worked alongside Sally for considerable time I have seen her utilise her coaching and training skills to transform those who are challenged in their role to become outstanding leaders. Her insight into the specific challenges faced in the emergency services industry easily relates to those she is training. I recommend that anyone new in a leadership role in emergency services undertake the specialised training that Sally offers. It's imperative to have teams working cohesively and all working towards the same goal... this is where Sally shines.

Sally Steward's innovative book, EMERGENCY SERVICE VOLUNTEERS: HOW TO GET THEM AND KEEP THEM, brings a whole new life to retaining volunteers in emergency services. Sally's in depth understanding of the challenges of volunteering has enabled her to have the greatest insight to assist organisations in keeping their most valuable asset... people. This guide is THE go-to book for anyone who works with volunteers on any level. Fantastic resource.

JARROD WINDON,
Rural Fire Service Queensland – Training Officer

Sally Steward has a passion for volunteerism and has both the experience and qualifications to offer her insights into recruiting and retaining volunteers. Sally's ideas, skills and professional approach to ensuring volunteers are valued and developed in their roles is an asset that all organisations should consider adopting."

CRAIG SMITH,
Superintendent, Emergency Management & Hazard Planning,
WA Dept Fire and Emergency Services

Sally is an amazing person who has integrity, compassion and extraordinary skills in understanding people who have been confronted with traumatic situations. Not only is she a good listener, but she helps people to move forward in a positive direction. Sally's focus is on helping others to become successful... I recommend Sally to anyone who wants to make the best in all facets of life by dealing with their stress in a constructive and useful way to prevent long-term impacts.

KAREN WEBBER,
Director at Equine Assisted Programs, Pty Ltd

Sally's unique understanding and compassion for all those who work in jobs that have high risk of stress, trauma or unsafe working environments makes her inextricably suited to assist these individuals to raise their Leadership and Resilience skills. Sally has heart, she has humour, she has skills/tools/technologies that are cutting edge to make long-lasting and powerfully positive changes both on a personal and business level. You will be astounded with Sally's generosity in spirit, knowledge and skills. I highly recommend Sally and urge you to have her on your 'team'.

DINA BONKE,
Partnership Manager at Institute of Public Works Engineering Australasia (NSW)

A remarkable insight from a truly remarkable leader. Sally Steward's ground breaking book: EMERGENCY SERVICE VOLUNTEERS: HOW TO GET THEM AND KEEP THEM, is an invaluable resource to retaining volunteers throughout all facets of emergency services. Sally's vast experience and unsurpassed professionalism as both a volunteer fire fighter and community educator make her the ideal mentor for volunteers and leaders alike. Her unbridled enthusiasm and sheer determination are what drives her pursuit toward developing strong and motivated leaders within the emergency services. This book is a vital asset to any person working with volunteers in any field.

MATT BENHAM,
Group Officer/Fire Investigator, Rural Fire Service Queensland

Sally's book, EMERGENCY SERVICE VOLUNTEERS: HOW TO GET THEM AND KEEP THEM offers a valuable insight into the role of volunteers within our community. With volunteers playing a major role in many organisations it is important to understand how to gain, train and retain volunteers. This book offers great suggestions in an easy to use format.

KERRYN GRESTY,
Senior Volunteer Learning & Development Officer
School of Fire and Emergency Services Training

I had the pleasure of working with Sally during the early days of her establishing her consultancy and never cease to be amazed at her ability to find solutions to problems that we all face in business.

If you get the opportunity to work with Sally, then I'd suggest jump at the chance.

DARREN RAMSEY,
Principal Consultant, Darren Ramsey Consulting

On a personal level Sally is both friendly and thorough in her approach, her attitude professional. I recommend Sally to anyone seeking practical strategies to overcome challenges in the workplace/emergency services.

FIONA DAVEY,
Tour and Event Manager

I have engaged Sally Steward on several occasions and have been delighted with the quality work. She is personable, professional and highly ethical in her approach. I am mostly impressed by the level of genuine compassion that she has shown me and her dedication to my results is outstanding.

SANDRA KELLY,
Owner Holistic Life Success

The most profound thing I have found with Sally is her genuine caring nature, she has shown me a wonderful quality of how to get really top notch results! Should you require an amazing woman with a genuine appreciation of her ability to help others to gain maximum results, I highly recommend Sally as being the Go-To Person!

BRET SOMMER,
Managing Director, World Enterprises (Group) Pty Ltd

Sally's involvement as a Rural Fire Fighter and Volunteer Community Educator Area Co-ordinator is outstanding. Her dedication and leadership qualities are utilised to mentor, train and support fellow volunteers. Sally understands the complexity of dealing with volunteers to get results.

This wonderful country of ours could not operate without volunteers. Sally's passion and communication skills are a perfect fit working and leading volunteers in any organisation.

GEOFF RICHARDSON,
Volunteer Community Educator Area Co-ordinator
Queensland Fire and Emergency Services

If you get an opportunity to work with Sally, take it now! Sally is incredibly in tune with and knowledgeable in all areas of leadership psychology. Professional and shrewd, Sally is a gem.

LUNE LIM,
Strategic Executive Officer, Aspire Developments

TABLE OF CONTENTS

ABOUT THE AUTHOR

SALLY STEWARD

A certified Performance & Master Results Coach and Master Practitioner of Neurolinguistic Programming, Sally Steward uses her extensive knowledge of Leadership, Business, Communication, Relationship Building and Emotional Intelligence to develop inspired, focussed and effective leaders.

Sally has been the CEO of businesses in the Construction, Property Education, Childcare and Online Retail Industries. She has also worked with eBay Australia as an Education Specialist and in the training departments of David Jones Australia, Department of Defence and Queensland Fire and Emergency Services.

As the owner and Senior facilitator of Leadership Emergency Services in Brisbane, Australia, Sally deals with the provision of training and coaching of leaders utilising experiential learning techniques and cutting edge training.

Sally's extensive experience and knowledge of Emergency Services was harnessed while working with Queensland Fire and Emergency Services in Volunteer Emergency Services Training,

Officer Development and Emergency Management. Sally's unique understanding in the emergency services industry has led to her specialising in leadership development, volunteer learning and engagement practises.

Sally is also an active Rural Firefighter and Volunteer Community Educator Area Coordinator as well as also having spent significant time leading disaster humanitarian relief volunteers to Fiji.

Sally's passion and excellence resides in Consulting, Training and Coaching on Leadership to develop amazing, strong and skilled leaders that are driven, focussed and inspiring.

MORE INFORMATION:

Facebook   www.facebook.com/sallystewardleadership

Web   www.leadershipemergencyservices.com

INTRODUCTION

Any organisation that relies on volunteers to operate has a huge task when it comes to recruiting, retaining and leading them effectively. All three of these components are linked inextricably and are crucial in having a highly valued, experienced and focussed volunteer workforce.

Not only is there a financial obligation in gaining, training and retaining volunteers, there is also a huge necessity to ensure volunteers feel valued, are making a difference and are being acknowledged for their contribution.

The first three months are recognised as the most critical time for retaining volunteers, with many leaving before twelve months as it's not what they were expecting or they don't feel as though they matter.

Many volunteer organisations rely on volunteer contributions to help them function effectively. While there are many roles a volunteer can play it's important to recognise that as people our strengths lie in the fact that we all have different interests, ambitions and skills.

Recruiting volunteers involves clear communication in both collaboration and information sharing, in conjunction with great leadership and role modelling. Not an easy task, nevertheless extremely rewarding for both the volunteer and the organisation when dealt with effectively.

This guide highlights some helpful strategies in recruiting new volunteers specifically for Emergency Services, along with leadership tips to retain your most highly valued assets... your volunteers, your people!

Cheers

Sally

The important fine print:

Although I have worked and volunteered extensively in the Emergency Services field, you need to know that any comments, views and information contained in this booklet are entirely my own and do not represent that of any Government or Non-Government Organisation.

PART 1

··

WHY RECRUITING
THE RIGHT VOLUNTEER
IS IMPORTANT

FINANCIAL AND OPERATIONAL NEEDS

Volunteers are priceless, we know that, but we should not ignore the financial impact they have on services and that volunteering does not come for free.

The classic volunteer of forty years ago was a housewife who had enough time available that she was able to commit to a regular schedule for her volunteering — four-to-six hours per week.

The volunteer of today is more likely to be employed, have professional skills to share, have a limited amount of time available, and have greater need for high personal reward. Today's volunteers want to see change happen quickly as a result of their contributions and are less likely to commit over a long period of time on a consistent basis.

LIKELY TO BE EMPLOYED

LIMITED FREE TIME AVAILABLE

GREATER NEED FOR PERSONAL REWARDS

HAVE SKILLS TO SHARE

Retaining volunteers has a hidden cost of time spent during induction... it's more an investment of senior volunteers spending additional time settling in the new members. From the standpoint of emergency service organisations the cost of recruiting and retaining volunteers is increasing. People are wanting more nationally recognised training and safety equipment is not only an expectation but a workplace health and safety requirement.

Organisations are constantly needing more people to fill their volunteer positions and they spend more time and money recruiting, organising, and effectively scheduling new volunteers. Since there are more volunteers required, the cost of training goes up aswell.

In order to maintain an effective and high quality volunteer program, staff and senior volunteers must dedicate time to communicate with and supervise volunteers. Staff, team leaders and others who directly supervise volunteers need to allocate time to provide training, day-to-day support and overseeing their role, in addition to interacting with and mentoring the volunteers.

Training Officers will often state that the best training is conducted on a one-on-one basis, with volunteers having an induction or orientation to the emergency service organisation. This is then often followed up with information on its services and then specific preparation for the responsibilities associated with their role.

FINANCIALS

The human connection of volunteering is costly, requiring a level of attention, caring and support.

With approximately 50% of volunteers becoming inactive within twelve months of joining an Emergency Services group, the financial loss can run into hundreds of thousands of dollars per year.

Providing new volunteers with full Personal Protective Equipment (PPE) alone costs on average $1,000 per person.

As an example, for every 100 emergency service groups who each recruit ten new members per year, a staggering $500,000 is lost in PPE costs alone.

EXAMPLE:

10 VOLUNTEERS
X $1,000 per volunteer
_____
= $10,000

X 100 EMERGENCY SERVICE GROUPS
in a region
_____
= $1,000,000

DIVIDED BY 50%
(volunteers who become inactive)
= $500,000 lost in PPE costs

OPERATIONALS

Even more important but not so easy to put a figure on, you have also lost:

> TIME (both administrative and operational)

> MENTORING AND ENGAGEMENT INITIATIVES

> TRAINING (external and in-house)

> SKILLS

> FRIENDSHIPS/TEAM MATES

> KNOWLEDGE GAINED

> EXPERIENCE

> OPPORTUNITIES

> RECRUITMENT AND PROMOTION

TOP TEN REASONS WHY VOLUNTEERS LEAVE

REASON #10

The reality of their experience is not what they expected when they signed on.

REASON #9

They don't like the work they are being asked to do nor how it is being done.

REASON #8

Veteran or leadership volunteers won't let them into the "insider" group.

REASON #7

They spend more time meeting than doing.

REASON #6

No one listens to their suggestions.

REASON #5

They feel unrecognised, and see that thanks are unfairly given to everyone, no matter who did the most work or none at all.

REASON #4

They are no longer asked to participate.

REASON #3

They do not actually understand how to get more involved.

REASON #2

They can no longer see how their involvement makes a difference.

AND THE #1 REASON VOLUNTEERS LEAVE IS:

It stopped being fun.

Source: http://criticalresponsenetwork.org/

PART 2

RECRUITING YOUR VOLUNTEERS

UTILISING RESOURCES:
SOCIAL MEDIA, ORGANISATION RESOURCES, WORD OF MOUTH, COMMUNITY EDUCATION

Recruiting volunteers can sometimes be a hit and miss approach with some units relying solely on word of mouth. While this strategy works well for some, there are many others that struggle with recruiting new members.

Most volunteer organisations have varied volunteer roles available utilising a lot of different volunteer skill sets. However, you still need to keep in mind that your volunteer needs to be a good match for the organisation.

THEY ALSO NEED TO:

> Understand expectations.

> Have patience during the recruitment process.

> Understand the training and attendance requirements.

> Abide by the code of conduct, procedures and policies.

PURPOSE

Understanding your new volunteer's purpose for joining your unit is essential.

DOES THEIR PURPOSE ALIGN WITH THAT OF THE ORGANISATION?

We all have a different reason or purpose for doing what we do. It may be to make a difference, save lives, or contribute to community safety. These would all align with an Emergency Services organisation, however if your volunteer's purpose is to "be a hero", or do things their way for example, then this isn't likely what your organisation wants to focus on.

If a potential new volunteer is only joining to gain free training and accumulate certificates, then that probably isn't in the organisation's best interests either. Maybe they are joining to get away from troubles at the last group or want to find that match made in heaven. Ask questions, be curious and look for the bigger picture. Will they be an asset to your team?

SO WHAT IS THE PURPOSE OF YOUR ORGANISATION?

Find out the Vision, Values and Purpose of your organisation and ensure that your existing team and any new members align with those ideals.

As an example: One particular Emergency Service uses the following statement, which underlies everything they do.

VISION:

Safe and resilient communities through partnerships.

PURPOSE:

To enhance community safety by minimising the impact of fire and emergency incidents on the people, the environment and the economy of Queensland.

VALUES:

> Customers first   > Empower people

> Ideas into action   > ZERO harm

> Unleash potential   > One Team

> Be courageous

Ensure your team, individual and organisational purpose are aligned and you will make the biggest impact, be the most effective and create the most growth in your Emergency Services organisation.

IN THE MEDIA

A media release (15 April 2014) from the Audit Office of New South Wales regarding the management of SES volunteers highlights some key improvements that all volunteer organisations could take into account. The Auditor General reported that:

"More needs to be done to retain Volunteers."

The Auditor General addressed the **high volunteer turnover** estimating that:

"Only half of the volunteers who join each year are active members 12 months later."

"....the SES should focus on recruiting volunteers that suit individual emergency unit's needs, improve induction and training, have clear pathways for volunteers to take on responsibility and improve consultation, communication and recognition."

"A charter for volunteers that clarifies roles and expectations would help."

CONSIDERATIONS

> Determine your unit's volunteer requirements. Are they support roles, operational, or related to community education?

> How many new members do you need?

> Do you have systems in place to support new members? (Mentoring, extra training, etc.)

> Are your members being recognised for their achievements, large or small?

ORGANISATIONAL RESOURCES

Many organisations already have resources in place to assist you to identify, plan and implement recruitment. Ask your organisation or marketing department how they can assist.

These resources can assist with organising, planning and implementing a recruitment campaign and are sometimes spaced over a set period of time, e.g. over a six-week period. They can include templates, instructions and ideas on utilising media, community and group members to recruit new volunteers.

OTHER IDEAS

PREPARING YOUR VOLUNTEER UNIT FOR RECRUITING NEW MEMBERS?

Prior to embarking on a recruitment drive your volunteer unit needs to assess its particular needs and readiness to incorporate new members.

Is your unit a place that is organised and has a happy and engaged culture, if not your members will see the upsets within and likely leave.

Having new members walk in the door is the final stage of recruiting volunteers; you need to do some groundwork of your unit and community first.

CURRENT MEMBERSHIP:

Look at your membership list, notice any members who haven't been to training or participated in unit activities for a while. Do they still want to be members, do they still live in the area? Having a clear idea of your unit's membership status will indicate if you need new members or you could engage and inspire the ones you already have.

How many members are active in your unit?

How many members have not attended or participated recently?

How many incidents and deployments did your group participate in, in the last 12 months?

How many senior members do you have available that could mentor new members?

Is the culture at your unit happy, engaged and supportive? ❏

YOUR COMMUNITY:

Is your community engaged in your volunteer service? Are there enough people living and working in the area to support it? Have a look at...

> Population growth

> Demographics

> Local businesses and clubs

> Other volunteer organisations

> Distance from other communities

YOUR UNIT'S PAST ATTEMPTS:

You have likely recruited new volunteers in the past, so how did that go? Are those volunteers still with you now? Have a look at what has worked for you in previous recruitment attempts and what hasn't worked. If your members left soon after joining, ask yourself why; was it the culture of the unit or was community support an issue? Do your members usually stay?

It could be many different things, but write them down so you are clear.

_____

_____

_____

_____

_____

BE SPECIFIC WITH YOUR UNIT NEEDS:

Having previously identified how many active members your unit has will assist in becoming clear on how many new members you need. Be realistic in your expectations as there is no point having 30 new members if you can only train and accommodate another five.

What specific roles are available at your unit? _____

_____

Do you have enough members to fulfil those individual roles?	❏
Do you currently have enough members to fully turn out to incidents?	❏
Does your unit struggle with retaining volunteers?	❏

ASSESSING THE CULTURE AND RESOURCES OF YOUR UNIT

SPACE AND RESOURCES

Volunteer units and their training facilities vary in size, space and fit out. Have a close look at the premises in which your new volunteers would be operating to ensure there are enough amenities, crewing vehicles, lockers and training space to accommodate them. You should also look at the financial capabilities of your unit to ensure that you can comfortably afford to fully recruit your identified number of new members.

SYSTEMS

You want new members coming into a unit that is organised and structured so they will have confidence in your professionalism. Routines and organisational information should be readily available, tidy and displayed. Look into what systems you have in place for the following:

> Communicating with members
  (Facebook, SMS, pagers, emails, etc.)

> Crewing days

> Rosters for maintenance, checks, cleaning

> Training calendar

> New member induction

> Office procedures

> Signing in/out

> Information sharing/notice boards

CULTURE AND MORALE

Volunteer organisations have a certain feel to people when they are in your company or visiting your unit. In determining your unit's culture and morale it is important to look closely at the following:

> What your current members believe about your organisation and about your unit?

> Listen to what they are saying when they think you are not listening. Is it complimentary and supportive of other members?

> Does it align with the values of the organisation?

> Are their comments solution based or based on blaming others?

Chances are that what your current members are saying to each other they are also saying out in the community and to their friends and family.

Having a unit with a negative attitude is not a good place for recruiting new members; they will feel the negative morale instantly. Listen to the attitudes of your members and be proactive in being solution orientated and creating harmony. Ensure you address these issues prior to recruiting new members. Leadership skills are addressed later in this book and will assist you in improving the culture and moral of your unit.

COMMUNITY PERCEPTION

Many of your volunteers will live locally and already be integrated into the community via their working life or recreational activities. Some may be members of local clubs, have children at local schools and owners or workers at local businesses. To raise awareness of your organisation, it is important for volunteer units to stay actively engaged in community life. Look at ways you can lift the profile and awareness of your organisation by:

> Attending and being active in local community events... offer your services

> Working with the media with stories of your unit's involvement

> Putting up organisational signage so people know where you are located

- Be active on social media... give tips, resources and information

- Get to know your local journalist, local newspaper editors and provide community minded stories

- Always be professional, positive and inspirational

WHERE TO FIND VOLUNTEERS

Having looked a little more closely at your local community, you will have already started to identify target areas. Here are a few more ideas:

- Past members
- Inactive members
- Local businesses
- Local clubs
- Truck drivers
- Skill specific
  e.g. Radio operator
- Groups with similar interests
- Suppliers
- Friends and work colleagues
- Councils

- Neighbours
- Major employers
- Landholders
- Senior students
- New residents
- Stay at home
- Self employed
- Farmers
- Seniors
- Community groups

When you are talking with members of the community interested in volunteering, think about why they would be motivated to volunteer.

Consider a targeted message that incorporates:

> Training and skills

> Making new friends

> Being a part of a team

> Being recognised in their community

> Saving lives

RESOURCES FOR YOUR RECRUITMENT CAMPAIGN

What resources does your organisation already have for inspiring and hiring new volunteers? Many organisations have this information printed and ready for you to use. However, someone with basic computer skills could also produce some paper-based materials:

> Brochures	> Banners	> Giveaways
> Posters	> DVDs	> Competitions
> Postcards	> Website	> Demonstrations
> Invitations	> Social Media	> Media releases

HEADING THE CAMPAIGN

Organising how and who will be taking responsibility for new member enquiries needs to be addressed prior to launching your recruitment initiative. This might be a mix of different people or one person depending on the needs and size of your unit. Carefully planning at this stage will enable a much smoother running process. Identify those in your unit that are experienced and would comfortably like to undertake…

- Phone calls and enquiries
- Note taking
- Record keeping
- Sales pitch — knowing exactly what to say*
- Speaking at information and training nights
- Interviews
- Answering questions
- Gathering information
- Follow ups and thank yous
- Facilitating events and community talks
- Putting up and taking down posters, etc.

Look for members who are inspiring, engaging and really have a passion for what they do. Ensure they embody professionalism and the values of your organisation.

*TIP: *You may not think that recruiting new members involves selling, however you are actually selling the opportunity to become a volunteer. Your sales pitch is instrumental in ensuring that you know what to say to potential new members and that you are getting your message across in a natural and engaging way.*

YOUR SALES PITCH

There is a simple sales pitch example that can help you. Answer each of the three questions in your own words, then combine the answers into your own sales pitch... keep it natural.

You might like to adapt the sales pitch examples below to suit your own organisation.

1 **What do you do as a volunteer?**

_____

_____

_____

_____

_____

> *E.g.* *"I help keep people safe by providing bushfire safety information and protecting property using fire management tools."*

2 **What my life was like before I became a volunteer...**

_____

_____

_____

_____

> *E.g.* *"I always felt that I wanted to do more with my life, learn new skills and give back to my community, but I wasn't quite sure how."*

3 What are the stand out features of being a volunteer...
what is it like now?

_____

_____

_____

_____

_____

E.g. *"Now that I am a volunteer at _____ , I have new friends,*
am an experienced fire fighter and I am continually learning
new skills. It's great being part of a team with a common focus
and knowing that I am making a difference.

4 Combine the above answers to create your personal sales pitch.

_____

_____

_____

_____

_____

_____

_____

_____

_____

_____

_____

STRATEGIES FOR RECRUITING

Getting the message out in the most efficient and effective way can vary between your unit's needs, the assistance available within your unit, your unit's financial situation and your community. Different strategies work in different circumstances, some suggestions:

KEEP IT SIMPLE - UTILISE EVERYONE, ALL THE TIME

Great for smaller units with limited amount of funds that require a quantity of new members. Recruiting can be something that is done continually over time making the most of opportunities as they arise. It is best that all your current volunteers have 'recruiting' as a focus when out and about in the community and when talking with individuals, always remembering to mention that their unit is actively seeking new members. Make the most of networking opportunities at community events, ensure you are visibly active in the community, and work with local newspapers and local business.

Considerations: Current members tire of continually promoting and can become complacent over time.

1. INVOLVE YOUR COMMUNITY

Creating an awareness of your volunteer organisation within your community and its requirement for new members requires that your community knows about it. One of the most effective ways to let people know you're on the lookout for new members is to utilise all resources at hand in a variety of ways over a set period of time. Preparation and organisation is key. Identify how you are going to use each resource. E.g. Posters in business and community windows, media releases to newspapers, letterbox drops, notice boards, banners and brochures at community events, unit training in the community, information nights and nominated contact person. Rather than involving the whole crew all the time, select members to undertake key roles and limit the timeframe for the recruitment to 6-8 weeks. Remember to ensure your roll out strategy is identified on paper so that you can keep track of names and contact details. You might consider one or more information nights to answer questions and provide further information.

Considerations: Be prepared for many enquiries and have a contact person and phone number on all your materials. Be realistic on the number of new volunteers you need.

2. PERSONALISED SELECTION

This is a 'by invitation' style of recruitment. Over a couple of weeks your current volunteers have brainstorming sessions listing as many people in the community that they believe have the skills and attributes required to fill the volunteer position. Businesses can also be identified that employ people who may meet these requirements. The next step is to invite the selected 'candidates' to an information night or community engagement event. This could be e.g. games night, fundraising night, and barbeque on a weekend, community awareness day or special open day. Show the invitees an exclusive view of your organisation and the opportunity to meet your team. You then have the opportunity to discuss the possibility of application for membership either at the event or with a follow up letter.

Consideration: Requires a personalised planning process and possibly catering. Be careful that your invitees aren't under the impression they are guaranteed membership.

3. POSITION TO BE FILLED

This low cost strategy looks at filling specific roles within the volunteer organisation. Ideally this works when you are looking at filling only a couple of vacancies and you are seeking people that have necessary skills and attributes to fill them. If you look at the skills required to fill a particular position you can then start targeting employers whose employees might be interested. Of course this would require discussion with management beforehand. Working with external organisations and building relationships can benefit the whole community.

A relative small volunteer organisation used this strategy to advertise six positions. Their advertising went like this, *"Six Fire fighter positions have become available at _____ Rural Fire Brigade. Please phone _____*

for a job description or more information. Applications close on _____ ". They only advertised through Facebook and had 40 applications.

Considerations: May require delivering a presentation at the external organisation and/or interview style applications.

FOSTERING A POSITIVE AND PROFESSIONAL ORGANISATION

Every time we put on a uniform, talk to our friends about being a volunteer, drive an organisation's vehicle or engage with the community, we are promoting that organisation. It's important that everything we do is fostering and promoting a positive and professional organisation. People buy what they *like* and people volunteer when they like what they see, hear and feel! What are you *selling* to the community?

THINGS TO CONSIDER:

› Looking professional — uniforms, public conduct and perceptions.

› Professionalism when communicating with the community.

› Promoting your organisation in a positive image — Social Media, word of mouth.

› Without realising it we are selling the image of a professional volunteer, be mindful of that always.

› Everything matters, even the small details

PART 3

....

RETAINING
YOUR VOLUNTEERS

VALUING AND KNOWING
YOUR VOLUNTEERS

Retaining a skilled and happy volunteer workforce is instrumental in ensuring your organisation fulfils its capabilities to the wider community.

As a leader at your group 75-80% of your time will be managing your members and potential new members.

Many people are put into leadership roles without understanding what is required, often thinking that training their team and ensuring they can do their job is their main role. As a leader you are not expected to know or do everything yourself, however it is important that you surround yourself with a great team that can support and provide assistance where needed.

Mentoring new members through the early months of volunteering is essential to ensure they feel included from day one. A mentor is most often someone that is a good fit with the new member, someone that they can easily relate to and feel comfortable enough to ask questions and seek guidance. A mentor doesn't have to be an expert on everything, they do however need to be resourceful so they can assist the new member and be able to offer guidance and support. A mentor will find out new member's goals and be there to help them achieve that.

> *Learning leadership skills is paramount to the success of your team. How can you influence people if you don't know what influences them?*

Ensuring volunteers are kept engaged and feel part of the team is extremely important in regards to retention. Allocating a mentor will help with this transition and assist in ensuring your new members feel as though their contribution is valuable and they integrate into the culture.

> *Consider a training and engagement schedule for new members while they are transitioning through the probation period.*

Are there training videos they can watch, online training they can participate in, skills they can read up on, policies and procedures they can familiarise themselves with? Are they invited to social gatherings so they can get to know members?

Look for ways for new members to feel part of the team while still complying with organisational policies. It will keep them from becoming bored and they will **feel like they matter:** both crucial aspects to consider regardless of where they are in the volunteering journey.

Getting to know your volunteers on a personal basis and having a good understanding of why they joined the group will aid in the success of them achieving their goals and keeping them happy and engaged.

> Is their purpose for joining in line with the unit's purpose of operating?

> Are you looking for a similar outcome?

People volunteer for many different reasons and dealing with someone whose main goal is to make new friends, as opposed to someone whose primary focus is to learn new skills, is likely to be very different.

WHAT DO YOUR VOLUNTEERS WANT FROM VOLUNTEERING?

SOME GOOD QUESTIONS TO ASK:

> What is it about volunteering as a firefighter or emergency service worker that interests you?

> Why did you join specifically?

> What do you hope to achieve as a result of being a member of this organisation?

> What are your expectations?

> What do you think it will be like?

> How did you find out about us?

> What are the things you would like to do or have an interest in learning?

> What are the things you do not want to do and are clearly off limits for you?

> Do you have any special needs or requirements?

LEADING YOUR VOLUNTEERS

Having successfully signed up new volunteers is fantastic, however, retaining them requires a multi-faceted approach, which includes effective leadership, role modelling, mentoring, training and team building.

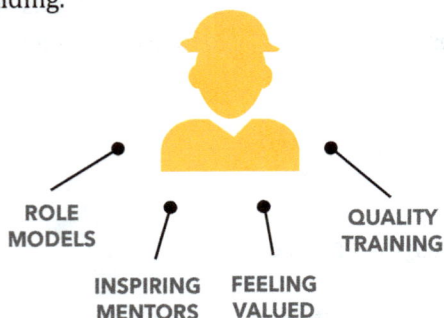

ROLE MODELS

INSPIRING MENTORS

FEELING VALUED

QUALITY TRAINING

ROLE MODELS

Success and professionalism of the group will be a direct result of the leadership you demonstrate in your role as Brigade Officer, Local Controller, Team Leader, etc. Members and volunteers will replicate and be an image of those that lead and manage the team. As an example, if your volunteers see that procedures and leadership is haphazard, then they in turn will become haphazard. This will create a culture of ineffectiveness throughout the unit; both in morale and professionalism.

Having a unit that values effective leadership, models professionalism and compliance with procedures will be shadowed in their members. The expectations of the volunteers and the group culture will reflect these qualities and as a result will be adopted by new members.

MENTORS

We all learn best when in an encouraging environment, which provides safety, certainty and the feeling our contribution matters. Ensuring new members have someone to confide in and learn from is imperative. Identifying those in your brigade who could be new mentors and are happy to fulfil that role will assist with retaining new volunteers. We all need mentors to succeed and learn from, so consider seeking a mentor for yourself and undertaking training to be an effective mentor.

ENSURE VOLUNTEERS FEEL VALUED AND MATTER IN YOUR UNIT

Get to know your volunteers and ask them why they have joined. Tailor their interests and skills to specific tasks, ensure they feel their contribution matters, say "thank you" timely and often!

If a member has joined to contribute more to their community they may feel satisfaction learning about Community Education and how they can pass on safety messaging. If they have a mechanical background their interest may lie with skills focussed around chainsaws and pumps, etc.

TRAINING

Are your volunteers trained so they can perform their duties effectively? Build their confidence and skills by providing an encouraging culture and ensure they can learn without the fear of feeling like they are a failure. Mix your training to cover skills and drills along with team building exercises. Ask your Training Officer for ideas and strategies to provide variety in your training. Keep it fun.

5 ESSENTIAL SKILLS FOR EFFECTIVE LEADERS

An Effective Leader is always thinking ahead, being an innovator and an inspirer, being encouraging and ensuring recognition for achievements. However, they are also a master of communication and engagement. The leadership skills identified below are essential for every effective Leader. While we may not be able to be everything to everyone all the time, we can always be mindful of our underlying intentions using the following as a guide:

SUSTAINABLE

INFLUENTIAL

ACCOUNTABLE

CLEAR

PRESENT

BE PRESENT

Being present is more than being in the same room, being present is your total engagement in a situation. This could be relating to your participation in a training exercise or even a conversation, however we also need to take into account other factors. Are you being fully present to the situations in your group and is there anything you are avoiding? When having conversations are you fully engaged or busy with your phone and easily distracted? Be present to difficult situations in your group... leaders don't avoid them. Be present to your responsibilities and those of your members.

There have been many difficult situations that could have been dealt with far more effectively if only the leader was truly present to the problem in the first instance.

ASK YOURSELF:

What is the one thing I am not being present to in my unit right now?

YOUR PRESENCE COULD INVOLVE:

> **ENVIRONMENT**: Turn phones off when in a discussion, be in a location where you will not be distracted. Give the member your full attention. Ensure team members feel **valued**.

> **TIME:** Allow enough time to deal with a situation so you can give your team member your full attention. Your time is a gift to your crew and will create **trust.**

> **AWARENESS**: Be present to group issues, deal with issues immediately and never turn a blind eye. Be aware of policies and procedures. Be present to member's achievements. Creates **respect and pride.**

> **PHYSICAL**: Be physically present, be part of member activities and lead by example. Be seen and be involved. Creates **team building.**

> **AVAILABLE**: Ensure your team knows they can come to you for anything. *Have an open door policy.* Creates a sense of security, **trust** and a feeling they are **valued.**

> **VISION AND VALUES:** Ensure you are present to the goals or achievements you want to reach as a group or unit, as well as the steps to reach these goals. What values are imperative in your group? What is your purpose? Collaborate on ideas, get your volunteers involved and encourage participation in group planning.

> **TRAINING:** Are you aware of training requirements and any shortfalls? Do your volunteers have a path to achieve? Do they know what is available to them? Volunteers want to learn, grow and be successful, as a leader you should be aware of how you can help them to accomplish that. *Be inspirational.*

BE CLEAR

Being clear involves our verbal communications (words), our instructions (MAP), intentions and expectations. If you aren't clear, people will do what they want because they are not sure what is required. This sometimes results in conflict, as volunteers may have not followed the correct procedure; however, consider that they also didn't receive the information that they require to undertake the task effectively.

WORDS:

Not only do we need to ensure the language we are using is appropriate, we also need to ensure that what we are communicating is being understood. Remember that is it is not the message sent that matters, it is the message received that counts. Consider the 7-35-58 rule.

1. The content (what you say) of your communication is only 7% of the actual message.

2. Your tone of voice (how you say it) represents 35% of the message.

3. Your body language (non-verbal) represents 58% of how your total message is received.

PLANS (MAP):

Your performance plans, group goals, training goals, fundraising goals and community education plans should all have a system of execution. Does your unit have a plan that is clearly identified to all group members?

Are your intentions and expectations on group matters clear to all members, even those who don't attend regularly? Relaying information to only a few people isn't being clear and you need a plan to effectively communicate group intentions to all members.

It may be that you don't have a plan on how to communicate correspondence to members, or you don't have a training plan for your members; look for ways that you can be clear and communicate your procedures. Consider putting systems in place so everyone knows what is expected.

INTENTIONS:

Are you being implicit or explicit in your intentions or communications?

Being implicit is giving vague instructions or without enough detail. As humans, some of us like lots of detail and some are comfortable with a big picture approach, however it is always important to be clear. Take into account that you may have new members who require more attention to detail while also having some that 'know the ropes', however it's your job as a leader to ensure everyone receives the same message.

Being explicit is determining exactly what is required, how to achieve it and by what time? "I would like all six hoses drying outside to be Dutch-rolled, put on the ladder truck in the next 30 minutes", as opposed to, "Roll those hoses and stick them on the truck". They might be asking which hoses, which truck and when do we do it!

EXPECTATIONS:

What are your expectations when it comes to your training, members, meetings, conduct, and attendance? You may already have an idea of what you expect, however, do your members know what is expected of them? Has this information been clearly communicated? New members often join up expecting one thing; however, they find out a few months down the track that it's not what they thought it would be like?

Is the information prior to recruiting new members clear and are their expectations aligned with what you deliver?

Being clear about volunteering responsibilities for new members and those who have been in the service for a longer period saves on many difficult situations down the track.

BE ACCOUNTABLE

As with volunteers, you are also representing your organisation in your actions or inactions. Ensuring your actions are ethical and that you are always role modelling in a positive manner promotes trust and respect.

If you are asked to do something and you habitually don't do it, your team will start to lose trust in you.

Follow through with requests?

Get back to people as promised and keep them informed?

> Does your team know that they can rely on what you say?

> Do you do what you say every time? (Saying one thing and doing another creates confusion and mistrust.)

We want to create trust, respect and confidence in our teams.

Remember a time when you heard someone say something and you thought, "That's rubbish, he/she is full of it!" That is lack of congruency and it is usually noticeable by those around you first.

People can tell when you aren't coming across as truthful and honest.

Be open about your actions, transparent in your dealings and if you make a mistake, be the first to acknowledge it. No one is perfect and it's ok to make mistakes; however, you will earn a lot of respect by taking responsibility for them, and doing so in a timely manner.

> Do your volunteers know the consequences if they don't follow procedures and policies?

> Are your volunteers accountable for their actions?

> Do your volunteers know what happens as a result of being more accountable and achieving their goals?

> Is there any reward system in place or a way you acknowledge their accountability or great work?

> Are you accountable for your actions?

> Are your dealings compliant with organisational policy?

> Are your dealings transparent?

> Does your team know the organisation's policies and consequences of not complying?

> If you are an Officer or Team Leader, do you know what your responsibilities are in relation to policies and compliance in your role?

What do you do as a group when a new member is successfully assessed on their initial training? Are they acknowledged?

Ensuring volunteers are accountable for their achievements engages them as they strive for success. Remember, when we were kids at school, we would strive for that gold star when we spelled

five correct words. Adults strive for success too and also like to be acknowledged for their achievements.

Whatever it is, we all want to be recognised and thanked for good work. We all want to know we matter.

BE INFLUENTIAL

Being a leader is about influencing others. So how can you influence someone if you don't know what influences them?

It's about engagement, not manipulation. It's much more effective to have your members following you because they trust and are inspired by you, rather than have the feeling you are spending all your time convincing and persuading them to do what you want.

Really knowing your members and having an understanding of what they are inspired by or like to do, will guide you to help them succeed in their aspirations.

> *Your job as a leader is to help others succeed.*

It's not about making people do things your way, it's about finding out what they want to do and helping them get there. For everyone this will be very different, however, assuming your way is the right way, is not an effective way to influence anyone.

To be truly influential your team must trust you, be proud and be inspired by you. Do you stand up for what is right, do they know you will take responsibility for them and back them 100%?

"Maslow's Hierarchy of Needs" depicts safety and belonging as prime human needs so you must ensure that your team knows they are safe in all respects.

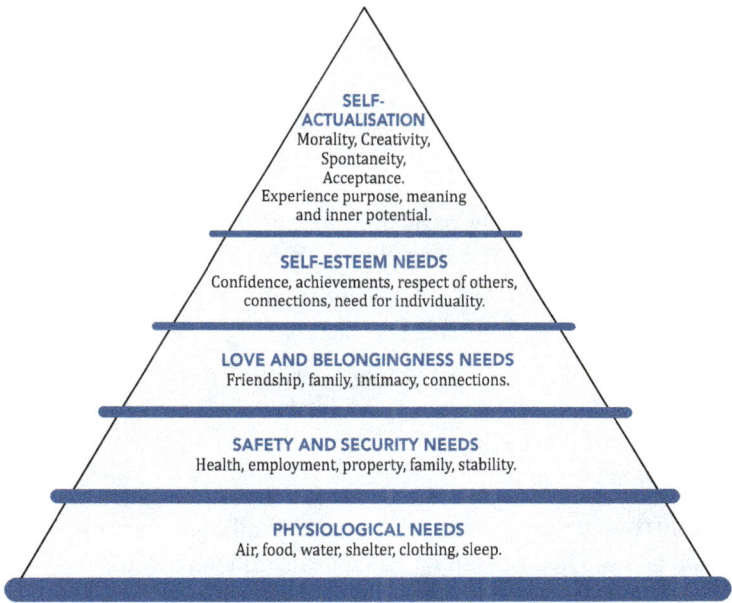

Maslow's Hierarchy of Needs

Leaders who take full responsibility for the actions of their teams and always recognise that they couldn't have achieved their success without the help of the group have the most respect.

Some leaders jump on the pedestal and relish in success, gloating that they did this and they did that and do not recognise the input or actions of their team. The same leader may also be quick to blame others if something goes wrong and is often the same person who will echo this to anyone who will listen. This creates a significant lack of trust amongst other members and shows a lack of integrity on the part of the leader.

RAPPORT

Building rapport is paramount for leaders and is something many do quite naturally. Building rapport is the basis of understanding human behaviour and body language. Appreciating that people operate quite differently is quite a good start. Some people are visual, some auditory, some auditory-digital and some kinaesthetic.

> **VISUAL:** These people learn and communicate more by imagining or looking at pictures. They picture things in their brain and learn by diagrams. They like seeing things drawn for them and most often recall details as a visual.

> **AUDITORY:** These people learn by hearing instructions. They prefer to listen to details and will relate details back by voice rather than in a written form. They will often repeat to you who said what.

> **AUDITORY-DIGITAL:** These people like detail… all the more the better. They will often relay information with all the specifications and more. They like forms, reporting and diarising information.

> **KINAESTHETIC:** Generally empathetic and a real people person. They are connected to their feelings and will tell you how they felt during an incident rather than the details.

SO WHY DOES THIS MATTER?

To really connect with someone and create rapport, it's important you are communicating with them in their own preferred representational system.

Imagine you asked a visual person to stand up in front of the group and talk about pump specifications and operations to the group during a training session. They may find this quite difficult, however if you asked them to draw a diagram on how a pump operates you will likely have more success, they are then able to relate visually.

Understanding how people tick is imperative in how you communicate with them and having an acceptance that everyone operates quite differently is also key.

COMPLIMENT PEOPLE

MAGNIFY THEIR STRENGTHS, NOT THEIR WEAKNESSES.

Think about your volunteers and how they like to communicate. Listen to how they talk to others. Is it about what they saw? What they heard? Is it about the intricate details or what they felt?

A Leader takes all the blame and none of the glory.

Find out why your new volunteers are joining. Is it new skills, community spirit, friendship, or excitement? Understanding this about your volunteers will assist in tailoring their volunteering experience and help them achieve their goals and provide rewarding experiences. It will also give you some guidance as to what roles they are more interested in and how best to work with them.

BE SUSTAINABLE

Leadership isn't something you learn, do once and it's complete. Leadership is a lifelong trait that many people already have. For some it comes naturally and others will learn the skills.

Being a sustainable leader is taking hold of the skills and transforming your team, inspiring those around you and helping people to grow.

You will create systems as part of your new leadership; they may be systems some of your team have helped to implement. Ensure the systems you have are for long term success and open to change and adaptation as time goes by. They should also be in the best interests of the unit and your team.

YOU MIGHT CONSIDER THESE SYSTEMS TO ENSURE SUSTAINABILITY WITH YOUR VOLUNTEERS:

> Measuring the success of your members.

> Members' individual achievements.

> Members' goals and training aspirations.

> Communicating brigade business to members.

> Training and mentoring new members.

> Members' attendance.

> Members who no longer attend.

> Fundraising goals.

> Brigade or unit three-year plan.

> Engagement practices for long term members.

> Agenda items for meetings called for prior.

Remember training and mentoring new members is costly and requires time and dedication. Ensure your systems address both new members and those who are long term members.

Recruiting and retaining your volunteers is a challenge and the success and effectiveness of your group is reliant on you creating great teams who stay for the longer term.

Training new members who leave soon after they receive membership or who rarely attend training and incidents are not sustainable practises. For your group to be sustainable, it is imperative that you are an effective leader, who has great teams and great systems.

Appreciation Strategy Humility
Commitment Responsibility
Integrity Leadership Listening
Honest Communication
Values Purpose Determination
Passion Principles

In any organisation there are three key areas: Money, Systems, People. You need to operate and be innovative with all three for your unit or organisation to be a success. Think of your unit as a business and look for ways to improve, grow and be sustainable in all three areas.

Remember you don't have to do this alone. Every leader needs help and should seek it. This help could come in the form of a mentor, a friend, a colleague or specialist in their field. Create great teams around you.

Be Curious
Provide Support
Embody Professionalism
Show Integrity
Be Grateful
Be Respectful
Be Fun

The resources and ideas provided to you in the book will be invaluable to you as a leader in emergency services. While we sometimes may be overwhelmed with the tasks before us as a leader, implementing just one or two of the ideas available to you will certainly put you on the right path. The largest transformations start with one small change.

If there is one aspect of this book that could significantly move you forward in your role I would suggest you 'be present'. Be present to your team, your obligations, your challenges and your purpose. Being fully aware of your responsibilities as a Leader and showing up each time to help others succeed will provide you with the most dedicated and passionate volunteers.

Take care, stay safe and thank you for doing all that you do.

Sally